knights

CONTENTS

knights

INTRODUCTION

On television there have been shows like "Knight Rider" and "The Blue Knight." They have not really been shows about knights. The word "knight" was used because the heroes of the shows were brave, good, strong, fair, and generous. The heroes fought the bad guys. That's the way we think about knights of the past.

Of course, we know there are no knights now. But at one time, there were real knights. They lived in Europe a long time ago. They were most prevalent from about 1100 to 1500.

In some ways, the knights were like soldiers and in some ways like the police. The knights knew the laws, and they ran the courts in the villages.

Most knights were strong and brave fighters. They followed rules or codes. They were fair in war. The knights were needed by the lords, the rich men who owned the land. They lived in castles on the land.

Most of the people of that time lived on farms or in villages. The villages were owned by the lords. There were very few towns or cities.

Most of the people were poor farmers. The lords let the farmers live in tiny houses on their land. In return for living on his land, the farmers gave the lord part of the food they raised.

Part of the knight's job was to protect the lord. To pay them for their fighting, the lord usually gave each knight a piece of land. Knights were very loyal to their lord. In return, the lord was generous to them.

Land at that time was passed on from father to son. The oldest son was given all the land. The younger sons were not given any land, and they were most often the ones who became knights.

Battles were not the same then as they are now. There were no great wars. There were no tanks, planes, guns, or bombs. Instead, the knights used horses, swords, daggars, axes, and lances. A lot of the fighting was man to man.

Knights were killed during battles, of course. But very often knights did not try to kill other knights. Instead,

ONE

THE TRAINING
OF KNIGHTS

Fathers often made plans early on for their baby sons to be knights. Starting at the age of seven, a boy trained for many years to become a knight. He was sent to his uncle's or a friend's castle. A young boy training to become a knight was called a page.

As a growing boy, a page spent a lot of time making his body strong. He ran and wrestled. He rode a horse, played ball, and bowled.

To train to be a knight, a page had to learn how to fight. He had to learn how to use weapons, such as a spear and sword. He had to learn how to be brave.

A page was sometimes taught to read and write. There were no schools, so lessons were given in the castle.

Like knights, pages were taught to be polite. They learned their manners from the lady of the castle. A page

A knight accompanied by trumpeters and his squire

had a busy day. He had to work around the castle. He had to set the table, light the candles, and serve the meals.

At the age of fourteen, a page moved to the next step in training. He became a squire. A squire trained to fight for hours every day. He learned how to use a lance while riding a horse. A lance was a long wooden pole with a sharp blade on one end.

As part of his training, a squire had to work for a knight. In some ways, he was like a servant. But it was an honor at the time to serve well. Priests served God, knights served the lords, and squires served the knights. The squire did many things for the knight. He woke the knight up in the morning and helped him get dressed. He served dinner. He took care of the horses and cleaned the stables. He took care of the knight's armor and helped the knight put it on, which was no easy task.

A squire went where the knight went. He went to tournaments, or war games. He handed the knight his lances and swords and helped the knight off the field if he got hurt.

A squire even went to war with the knight and sometimes fought. Squires were paid to go to battles but were paid less than knights.

A squire's life wasn't all work. He learned how to play music, sing, and dance. He learned these things to win the love of a lady.

When he was twenty, a squire was allowed to become a knight. But first he had to find a lord to serve, and he needed a lot of money. He had to get the things a knight needed—horses, clothes, armor, and weapons. All these things were very expensive.

DUBBING ➤ There was a special ceremony when a squire became a knight. The ceremony was called "dubbing."

There were many things a squire had to do before the ceremony. First, he took a bath. Bathing was a sign that he was pure. Sometimes he trimmed or shaved his beard and his head. Sometimes he cut off only a small piece of hair. Cutting his hair was a sign that he would honor God.

The squire spent the night before the ceremony in church. He stood or knelt all night at the altar. The squire was told to think about being a knight. A knight had to live by a code or set of rules. He had to fight for good causes. He had to believe in God. He had to learn to deal with bad luck. He had to be good to his friends and brave in front of his enemies.

The dubbing ceremony was very solemn. The squire wore special clothes for the event. He dressed in different colors. Each color was a sign or symbol. A white tunic or shirt showed that the squire was pure in spirit. Black stockings and shoes showed that he was not afraid

A knighthood is conferred.

to die. A red cloak was a sign that he was willing to shed his blood in battle.

The ceremony took place outdoors. Music was played. Flags were flown. The knights and ladies in the lord's castle gathered. They wore their finest clothes. Then the squire kneeled before the lord. The lord tapped the squire on the neck or shoulder with a sword and said, "I dub thee knight." The squire was now a knight and given the title, Sir.

Before and after a dubbing, there was always a big party. There was eating, singing, and dancing. Sometimes a squire was dubbed around a holiday like Christmas or Easter.

There was a quicker way to become a knight. Sometimes during a battle, knights were needed immediately. There was no time for a special dubbing. The squire was just told, "Be thou a knight." For a poor squire who didn't have much money, that was a way to become a knight.

The sword was worn in a case fastened around the waist. It hung on the left side. On the right side of his body, a knight wore a dagger or knife.

Knights used lances. The lances were long and came in many sizes. Knights also used axes and maces. Maces were wooden clubs with spikes stuck into them.

ARMOR AND SHIELDS ➤ Knights needed to protect themselves during battle, so they wore armor and carried shields.

At first, the armor was made out of small metal rings. That kind of armor was called chain mail. The metal rings were put on leather or cloth coats. The rings were also put on pants and boots. A suit of armor could have more than 200,000 rings!

But chain mail was heavy and uncomfortable. It was often hard to move in it. Also, arrows or other weapons could hit the spaces between the rings. Even with the heavy woolen pads they wore under the chain mail, the knights could get seriously hurt.

Eventually, knights covered their entire bodies with plates of metal. There were plates covering the chest and back, the arms and legs. There were even metal gloves. A metal helmet protected the head. The knight could bring down a metal cover, or visor, over his face, hiding himself completely.

Hinges were made so that the knights could bend their arms and legs and move their fingers. To move more easily, a knight needed to oil his armor.

A suit of armor was very heavy. It weighed between forty and sixty pounds. It was also very hot and uncomfortable to wear. But at least it protected the knight.

Shields were made of wood or metal. A knight held a shield in front of him during a battle to block swords or other weapons.

Knights often put designs or emblems on their shields to show who their families were or who their lord was. The designs were often pictures of flowers and animals. Different colors were used as symbols. Each family had its own emblem.

Sometimes the emblems were sewn on the coats the knights wore over their chain mail. This became known as the "coat of arms."

If you go to a museum, you may see armor and shields. You can pretend to be a knight, wearing armor and carrying a shield into battle.

HORSES ➤ Knights were fighters on horses. It was the horse that made the knights different from foot soldiers. Most knights owned three horses. Two horses were used for day-to-day jobs and one was used for wars. A war-horse cost at least four times as much as a workhorse because it was trained better than the other horses. It was also bred for size and strength, stamina and courage. It was trained to trot when the knight gave it signals with his legs. The war-horse did not gallop because it was hard to ride a horse while wearing so much heavy armor.

A knight took very good care of his horses. He fed them before he himself ate. He gave water to his horses before he took a drink for himself. He even let his horses sleep in his tent. To protect the horses, the knight put armor on them also.

three

CASTLES

Knights lived in homes called castles. Castles were built to protect the lord, his family, and his knights. They were often built on hills so the knights could see a long way off. That made it hard for enemies to sneak up on the castle.

The castles were usually made of stone. Some of the walls were 20 feet (6 m) thick. Some castles were as high as 80 feet (24 m). That's as tall as a building with eight floors! Some castles were 700 feet (213 m) long; that's as long as a city street.

Large castles had many towers, the largest of which was called a keep. Under the keep were dungeons, or prisons. The floors of the castle had trapdoors which opened up. Those who attacked the castle would fall into the dungeons below when they stepped on the trapdoors.

Knights of medieval times lived in castles.

The castles were surrounded by walls. There were no trees in front of the walls, so no one was able to hide. On the top of the walls were places to walk or run. The knights fought from there. There were also holes in the walls through which the knights shot arrows. These were called "murder holes."

Many of the castles had moats around them. A moat was a deep ditch filled with water. There was a drawbridge going across the moat. The bridge was kept up until a person in the castle needed to cross the moat. Then the bridge was lowered.

BATTLES ➤ Castles were sometimes under attack for months or even years. The first attacks were made by the men called foot soldiers. They were the poor soldiers who did not own horses. After the foot soldiers started fighting, the knights attacked. The knights only took part in hand-to-hand fighting.

The foot soldiers had a very hard job. They were hurt or killed more often than the knights. To help them in their attacks, the foot soldiers had all kinds of weapons and machines. Machines called catapults were used to throw large rocks over the walls. Battering rams (ancient machines used to batter down walls) were used to punch holes in the walls. There were towers called cats. The cats had wheels that were rolled up to the wall. The foot soldiers climbed up the cats and tried to go over the castle wall.

four

LIFE IN
THE CASTLE

A castle was a damp and dirty place. In the winter, it was cold since there was no heat except for fireplaces. In the summer, it was very hot. The castle did not have many windows, so it was dark, too. The few windows were small holes in the walls covered with thick paper.

In the center of the castle was a very large room called the hall. That's where almost everything was done—meals were eaten, trading and business took place, parties and feasts were held.

Large tables were set up in the hall for meals. The lord sat at the center of the table. The knights slept in the hall, too. Only the lord had a bedroom of his own. In the larger castles, the lord and his lady had a bedroom upstairs. The only pieces of furniture in the room were a bed, a chest to keep clothes in, and a chair or two.

*The inside of a castle in the fifteenth
century looked like this.*

Like all the rooms in the castle, the hall was lit with candles or oil lamps. It was heated by a fireplace. Some fireplaces were huge and whole trees could be burned in them.

When flowers were in bloom, they were placed on the floor of the castle to help make the air smell better. The air was stale from the smoke of candles and fireplaces.

The lord's bedroom didn't have very much furniture in it.

Rugs were put not on the floors but on the walls. They helped keep out the cold air. The people put animal skins on the walls, too.

There were no bathrooms like ours in castles. The people used big pots called chamber pots instead of toilet bowls. Instead of toilet paper, straw was used. Tubs made out of wood were used for bathing. The tubs had a seat where the knight sat while his squires poured water over him. The knights and the lords did not take a bath every day. They took a bath once a week, sometimes less often. They liked to rest in the tub. The baths helped make their bites from fleas, lice, and insects feel better.

After their bath, the people put their dirty clothes back on. They did not wash their clothes very often. They had to wash the clothes in tubs or streams, and there was little soap available.

There was a kitchen in the castle, but it was not like our kitchens today. The cooking was done over a roaring fire in a large fireplace. Near the kitchen was a garden where herbs, fruit trees, and vegetables were grown.

All things had to be made by hand or grown. There were no stores to go to to buy food or other items. All the food was grown in the fields, and animals were raised for meat. Clothes and shoes and tools and dishes and ropes and weapons—everything was made by hand.

It took a lot of people to do all the work in the castle. There were people to make the candles, wash the clothes,

Taking a bath in the time of the knights was quite different than it is today.

A kitchen scene during medieval times

During medieval times the people had to produce all their own food, including baking bread.

and prepare the food. There were even people to cut hair. The hair cutters also pulled teeth!

There were people who took care of the horses and stables, others who worked in the gardens, and others who helped the lord and his lady. A steward was the person in charge of all the workers at the castle. He had to learn what things cost, how to keep track of the food, and how to get everything done. He also had to make trades. He had a very important job.

five

A DAY IN
THE CASTLE

A day in the castle started when the sun came up. Everyone washed with cold water and got dressed.

Men wore pants, long socks, and tunics, or long shirts, with sleeves. Over the tunics, they wore shorter tunics without sleeves. The tunics were blue, yellow, purple, green, or red. They were made of wool or, for the rich knights, silk. At that time, cotton was for the rich, too, because it took a long time to make cotton by hand.

Women also wore tunics. They put on simple dresses over the tunics. For parties and special occasions, they wore long dresses with flowing sleeves. Unlike today, dresses were kept for years and years. The ladies wore gold dust or gold nets in their hair for decoration.

It was the style at that time for women to make their faces look very pale, so they wore white makeup. It was made of sheep fat.

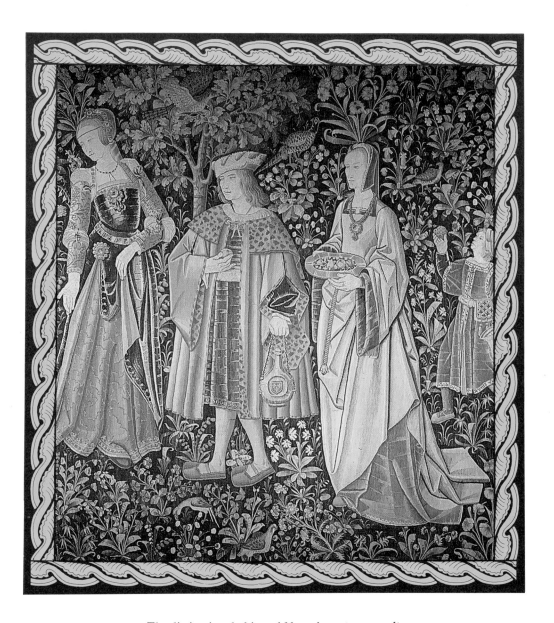

The distinctive clothing of fifteenth-century royalty

Inside the castle, people wore slippers. Outside, they wore boots. The knights wore purses on their belts because there were no pockets in their pants. Their clothes were held on by pins because there were no buttons. The knights and their ladies liked jewelry and jewels. They liked to wear gold pins, chains, and rings. They put jewels on just about everything, even their gloves.

After getting dressed, the knights had a light breakfast. Then they fenced or rode their horses. The pages and squires had their lessons. The girls had lessons also. Like the pages, they were sent away from home at the age of seven. They learned how to read and write. They also learned how to run the castle when the men were away at war.

Between ten and twelve in the morning, everyone ate. Before the meal, the knights washed their hands. They liked to add perfume to the water. The midday meal was a very large one that lasted for hours. For the main part of the meal, meat and bread were eaten. Whole cows, pigs, or deer were cooked at one time. That was what knights liked to eat best. Poor people rarely ate meat. Instead, they ate bread or porridge, sometimes chicken. There were no refrigerators or ice during those days, so meat was often salted or smoked to preserve it.

Fish was eaten if there was a pond or river close to the castle. People also ate all kinds of birds and put whole

*A meal being served to the lord's
residents of the castle*

cooked birds inside pies. They served pretty birds like peacocks with the feathers still on as decorations.

The knights ate very few vegetables. They liked peas, onions, and beans best.

Meat was often boiled or roasted on spits. Fat was not used for cooking because it cost a lot. Fat was used to make candles and soap. There was not enough of it for cooking, too. A pound of fat cost four times as much as a pound of meat.

Just like us, the knights liked desserts. They used honey for many of their desserts. They liked fruit cooked in honey. They made pies out of the fruit. They did not think raw fruit was good for them. They ate cookies, cakes, and waffles, too. These items cost a lot to make because sugar was not easy to buy. Sugar came from far away and was very expensive.

During holidays, the people ate even more! All work stopped. Everyone in the castle ate and drank for up to fourteen days. People drank a lot of wine and beer because the water was not clean. Milk was not always good to drink either. There was no way to kill the germs in it as we do today.

Food was served on plates made of wood, but two people used the same plate. Sometimes instead of a plate, the knights used day-old bread to put their food on. They finished the meal by eating this bread-plate!

People ate food with their fingers. Forks were not invented yet, but people did use spoons for soup. It sounds as though the knights did not have any manners, but they did have rules. They were not allowed to put their elbows on the table, for instance. They were not allowed to burp. They were not allowed to stuff their mouths or wipe their mouths on the cloth covering the table.

After eating, games like chess were played. Chess was played both for fun and to give the knights a chance to plan actual fighting moves. The chess sets were sometimes made of silver. The knights also loved to play games they could bet on. They loved to bet their money or gold.

The knights liked to hunt. The lord usually set aside large areas of land for this. There were strict rules about hunting deer, wild pigs, and rabbits. The men hunted foxes and wolves. They used nets and bows and arrows and spears to hunt. They trained their dogs to hunt, too. Many knights trained falcons for hunting. The falcons were taught to hunt other birds. They were difficult to train. The knight would wear a hard leather glove and carry the falcon on his wrist. The falcons were called "birds of the fist."

After hunting or playing, the knights had a light meal in the late afternoon. During the meal, they told jokes or stories or sang songs. Many of the knights made up their own songs. After the last meal, the single knights and ladies sang and danced. Sometimes singers, dancers, joke

Hunting with falcons was a favorite pastime.

One form of entertainment was singing and dancing.

tellers, and dog trainers came to the castle to entertain. They went from castle to castle and town to town. Storytellers went from castle to castle, too. At an exciting point in the story, the storyteller would stop. Naturally, everyone wanted to know what happened next. But before the storyteller would go on, the people had to pay him. Most of the stories told were true tales, but often the storyteller made the story of a battle a little more exciting than it really was or made a love story a touch more romantic.

SIX

WAR GAMES

The two knights climb up on their horses. They pull the visors of their helmets down over their faces. They spur their horses, and the horses charge toward each other. The knights aim their lances at each other. A hit, right in the chest! The knight on the brown horse is knocked off, but he isn't hurt. After all, it's only a game.

Knights loved such war games, or tournaments. These tournaments were held for two reasons. One reason was to give the knights a chance to train for real wars. In some ways, it was like the training of today's soldiers. The second reason was that the knights enjoyed these games. They were a way to have fun and to show off their skills.

For the tournaments, the knights used swords and lances with dull edges. Sometimes they used maces.

The beginning of a tournament

At first, the war games were wild. They were like free-for-all fights. The knights met at a field near a castle and called sides. They lined up on two sides behind ropes. When the ropes were cut, they charged at each other. They hit each other with their lances, and the fight began. The fight lasted from early afternoon until dark.

There was a part of the field where the knights were able to rest for a while. That was the only place where fighting was not allowed.

There were no other rules in tournaments. There were no judges and no points. The knights did what they wanted. The winners were the knights left standing at the end of the game. Because there were no rules or judges, many knights were accidentally hurt or even killed.

Over the years, the war games changed. They were not so wild anymore. There were judges, and points were given. Rules were set up. You could not hit anyone from behind or hit anyone who had lost his helmet. You could not hit a horse. You could not use sharp weapons or hit below the waist.

If knights broke the rules, they lost points. Sometimes they were thrown out of the games. If they were very bad, they had their horses taken away or they were sent to prison.

The knights loved to capture other knights. Sometimes the captured knights tried to get away, although at times it was against the rules to do this. The ones who were caught often had to pay to become free again.

Not all knights were allowed to take part in the contests. Those who had stolen something, those who were not polite to ladies, those who had deserted a battle, those who had sold things to make money, and those who had destroyed crops were kept out of the war games.

The war games changed more and more over the years. Soon they were like a party. Many times they were held during a wedding or holiday feast.

Stands were built where the knights, ladies, and lords watched the contest. The stands were hung with drapes to keep the sun off the crowd.

The ladies enjoyed the war games as much as the men. Often a knight fought in honor of the lady he loved. A knight liked to wear a scarf or ribbon given to him by his lady. It was a great honor to be picked by the ladies to open the war games.

Before the tournament, the knights put their armor on display. They wore their full set of armor and put armor on their horses, too. The poor horse—its armor and the knight's armor weighed up to 160 pounds! Because of the heavy load, the horse was not able to gallop; it could only trot.

In time, the contests between two knights were what the crowd wanted to see most. Such contests were called jousts. They were games of skill, not murder. Each knight was matched against a knight with similar skills.

The goal of the joust was to knock the other knight off his horse. The knights were placed on either side of a rope. A piece of cloth was hung from the rope. In later years, a low fence made of wood was put between them. That helped to protect the knights and their horses.

*Jousting contests were games of
skill between knights.*

When a horn was blown, the knights rode their horses toward each other. They rode slowly and held their lances in their right hand. They tried to hit each other on the head or chest.

Over the years, saddles and stirrups were made stronger and better. That made it more difficult to knock a knight off his horse. It became a real thrill for the crowd when a knight was finally knocked down.

Scores were given for the jousts. A knight was given three points for knocking the other knight off his horse. He was given two points for breaking his lance on the other knight's shoulder or helmet and one point for hitting the other knight above the waist.

The knight who won kept the horse and armor of the knight who lost. The losing knight sometimes paid to get his armor and horse back. The winners of the jousts were given prizes, too, things like meat or fish or a piece of armor. At contests given by very rich lords, the knights were given jewels as their prize. Knights who were poor tried very hard to win because that was a way to become rich.

Jousts did not always take place as part of the tournaments. There were many kinds of jousts. There were even "jousts of war." They were used to settle fights. Sharp weapons were used, but both knights had to agree on which ones. These contests were often fought until one knight was killed. Sometimes a judge stopped the fight.

Knights sometimes took part in a "feat of arms." This was three or four contests usually between the same two knights.

The tournaments became big and fancy and took months to plan. At the same time the war games were put on, parties were held. There were great dinners or feasts, singing and dancing. The knights and ladies wore their best clothes and jewels.

The contests often started on a Monday and ended

on a Thursday. The church did not allow contests on Friday, Saturday, or Sunday. At times the church did not want the knights to have the contests at all. This was true during the years when many knights were hurt or even killed.

seven

CHIVALRY

Knights were expected to live by a strong, strict code. They were expected to fight for their lord and be loyal to him. They were expected to serve the church and God. And they were expected to take care of their ladies. This code was called chivalry.

But what were knights *really* like? There were very few knights who were able to live by this code all of the time. They were more interested in fighting and getting rich. In short, knights were far from perfect.

Knights were often vain. That made them do foolish things like fighting for silly reasons. They fought to prove their lady was pretty. Or they fought anyone who said something bad about her.

Once in a while they fought even when there was no chance of winning. Knights sometimes wanted to fight so

Pope Urban II preaching during the First Crusade

much they began a battle on their own. They did not wait for the order to charge. They ruined the leader's plan and then they lost.

Even in their service to God, the knights were not always good. When Pope Urban II asked them to win Jerusalem from the Muslims, thousands of knights went there. They fought hundreds of battles during the religious expeditions called the Crusades. During the Crusades, there were knights who killed whomever they found, even women and children. The knights destroyed the land and villages and stole from the Muslims.

According to their code, the knights were expected to take care of the ladies. They treated their sweethearts and rich women well. But often they did not treat the poor women as well. They did not treat their wives very well either, for married women had very few rights.

A knight usually did not marry for love. His parents told him whom he had to marry. Sometimes he married to stop wars between lords. Sometimes he married because the woman's father offered him land as a wedding present.

As part of their code, the knights tried to prove they were good enough for their ladies. They fought many battles. Sometimes a knight wore a patch over one eye until he did something brave. Sometimes he wore a piece of lace on his shoulder until he was in a battle. Then he gave the lace to his lady.

King Arthur ruled England long ago. He had a great, magical sword called Excalibur, and he lived in Camelot. He was brave and good and wanted to rule the land fairly. He gathered loyal knights together and asked them for their help. King Arthur and his knights began the Round Table. They joined together to make rules and protect the country.

Other stories tell about knights fighting fire-breathing dragons and rescuing beautiful ladies. There are tales about knights finding wonderful treasures, fighting witches and monsters, and falling in love.

It is easy to see why there are so many stories and poems about knights. The stories usually make life in the days of knights seem very romantic. In some ways, of course, they were. As you have read in this book, though, life in the days of knights was not always romantic or easy. But it was sometimes very exciting.

FOR FURTHER READING

Gibson, Michael and Trisha Pike. *All about Knights*. New York: EMC, 1982.

Glubok, Shirley. *Knight in Armor*. New York: Harper, 1969.

Hindley. *Knights and Castles*. New York: EDC, 1976.

The Knights. New York: Arco, 1979.

Windrow, Martin. *The Medieval Knight*. New York: Franklin Watts, 1985.

INDEX

ABOUT
THE AUTHOR

Carole Lynn Corbin, formerly a research librarian, is the author of several books for teenagers. They include *John Lennon, The Right to Vote, A Picture Album of Television,* and *A Picture Album of the Sixties.*

She also wrote a high interest/low vocabulary book, *Stunt People and Stunt Work,* which was chosen by *Booklist* as one of the year's best. She was the video consultant for the magazine *School Library Journal.* She is the compiler of *Short Stories on Film and Video* and the editor of *Children's Media Marketplace.*

Ms. Corbin has written many articles on a wide variety of subjects: computers, flying, women's rights, cable television, the origins of everyday objects, unique inventions, movies, and television. She has also interviewed many celebrities, among them Jim Henson.

She lives in New Jersey with her teenage son, Scott.